PERSONS, PLACES,
& THINGS

ALSO BY ARLENE POLLACK

Flamencos

PERSONS, PLACES, & THINGS

Selected Poems

❖

Arlene Pollack

FCP

Full Court Press
Englewood Cliffs, New Jersey

First Edition

Copyright © 2013 by Arlene Pollack

Published in the United States of America by Full Court Press, 601 Palisade Avenue Englewood Cliffs, NJ 07632 www.fullcourtpressnj.com

ISBN 978-1-938812-24-8
Library of Congress Control No. 2013955521

Editing and Book Design by Barry Sheinkopf for Bookshapers (www.bookshapers.com)

Cover photograph, "Marsh Bridge," Copyright © 2008 by Howard Pollack

Colophon by Liz Sedlack

TO HOWARD MERRILL POLLACK

my lifeline, my love,
my lucky charm

To our six children and their mates
our eleven grandchildren and great-grandchild
our nieces, nephews, cousins
and dear friends

This book belongs to each of you, as do I

ACKNOWLEDGMENTS

I want to thank Howard, whose loving help has always meant so much to me, and my family, for enriching my life.

I also want to express my appreciation to Dr. Arline Lowenthal, for her encouragement and for suggesting the title of this book; to Barry Sheinkopf, whose support led me to gather my thoughts onto these pages; and to the parents who gave me up for adoption at birth: I understand.

TABLE OF CONTENTS

ADOPTED

Knowing full well my search would lead nowhere,
With eyes veiled to conceal my interest,
I have looked for Mother in places known and rare.

At first I sought her in those places where
My heart felt most at home, yet, all the while,
Knowing full well my search would lead nowhere.

One summer in Rome, I thought I'd seen her there,
Retraced my steps to find her shop; could not.
I have looked for Mother in places known and rare.

I have looked for Mother deep within my heart,
Studying myself, the children I have borne,
Knowing full well my search would lead nowhere.

In my travels, making time to spare,
I have searched through records, for what I do not know.
I have looked for Mother in places known and rare.

I have not found my mother anywhere;
Yet she has never once been lost to me:
Knowing full well my search would lead nowhere,
I have looked for Mother in places known and rare.

Then

I HAVE SOMETHING TO SAY

(To Howard Pollack)

I want to speak of living past
our prime, then making up a life
devoid of work, of paychecks,
and of schedules imposed,

of being there where life exploded
into a million fragments of emotion,
and how we thought up strategies
to win the war.

I want to speak of living in the past,
the present and the future all at once,
without uneasiness or strain,

of knowing things we once surmised
but didn't trust to be, of traveling
great distances in one small space
and thinking it enough, that solitude,
that power, that sheer love of life
that once seemed unattainable.

I want to speak of living hurried up,
examining in depth one last important time.

I want to speak of who you are to me

and I to you and who we are together
in this space of time before we close.

I want to speak of how we grew into
each other, how we came to be the
family's core, one cohesive life
from such unruly weeds,

how we feel within us something powerful,
and how we see the picture, not the
fragments of this odyssey.

While the days go by, spinning us
into eternity, I want to say *hello,
goodbye, I love you, thank you for
this poem.*

MODERATION

Everything in moderation,
Mother says, working at the
tangled skein of yarn.

I dance away, pull the yarn
behind me, unravel the ball
she's made of nothing usable.

Fifty years go by. The yarn's
run out. I hold one end and
she the other. We start
skeining it again, come
closer, closer, drop our
balls of yarn worn thin as
rag, yet strong as steel.

Sitting face to face, I bent
around myself, she bent
forever bow-like, together we
start raveling.

Everything in moderation,
Mother whispers, working at
her length of tangled yarn.

I nod my *yes*

and, eager for the patching,
hold my skein in readiness.

NEXT ROOM

1.

My father
is lying face-brown-as-a-nut up,
his nose carved out of the bones
of his face, brown skin
stretched taut.

My father's eyes
are in their hollow sockets,
looking anywhere.

I bend
to kiss the sweat-beaded forehead
where the white hair falls in
feathers over the sockets,

and then
my father clutches my fleshy
pink arm with his pink-nailed,
blue-veined claw.

There is, he says, *something*
for you in the next room.
Yes, I say into the eye sockets,
wishing the claw looser.

There is something, I say!
he says, *in the next room!*
He is angry and senile, or
angrily senile.

There is something, I say,
he says, *in the next room!*
I know, I say.

THERE IS SOMETHING . . .
He jerks his head around,
positioning his sockets to face mine,
. . . IN THE NEXT ROOM, YOU FOOL!

I SAY I know.

Next room is wraiths
with brown nut faces, waiting
for removal.

My father dies.
My arms float free
and I expect no more
from Father.

2.

I am beginning my brown nut-faced
being with claws that grip

which used to stroke.

My grin is ghoulish in the mirror
or a yellow slash in repose.
I look to see what still
remains of pink soft roundness.

I see my father.

See? he rasps, *I told you
there is something in the
next room.*

Yes, I say, my eye sockets
fixed on his eye sockets,
my claws gripping the
dresser mirror

in whose reflection I see
my father's tobacco jar,
brass badge, the old billy club
and silver whistle.

My face in the dusty mirror
has become jawless, my mouth
pursed in an uncommon frown.

The nostrils of my beak
are long and furry,
the skin stretched over it

taut as a surgeon's glove.

I found it, there on the
shelves, I tell him.
You're not so dumb, he says,
and fades into the mirror.
Not anymore, I say to myself
into which he has retreated.
I call San Diego,
Andover, Moonachie,
call up three
flights of stairs, the phone
gripped in my bony claw.

There is, I say, *something*
for you in the next room.
Yes, they say, with pansies
in their throats. *We know.*
THEN GET IT NOW, I hiss,
pulling on the wire
to draw them in.

DON'T BE FOOLS, I say.
They say all right, they'll come.
You'll come together?
My asking sends long thin wails
through the wire.

We'll come. We'll come.
We'll come, echo the

voices carrying my blood.

In the glass my father nods.

TULIPS

Against the closet door
My father bangs my head
In rhythm with his fury.
I beseech the tulips:
Do something!

Behind, but not intruding,
Mother stands.
The tulips wink:
We're watching.

I address the tulips:
You have led me to believe . . .
They are implacable.

Ten seconds
His fists pummel
As my head collides
With closet door,

She standing silently,
Her face in shadows,
While the tulips stare
From all directions.

Now, at last,

She mews in protest:
Julius. Only that.

He stops abruptly
And they disappear,
Leaving me to muse on it.

From where I lie
The tulips speak in unison:
It is a sunny day!
Get up!

I answer slowly, wondering
What crime has been committed.
I must be to blame.

Why else? the tulips hiss.

YOU AND I

(To my father)

I remember, Dad,
your calling down the corridor
lined with wheelchairs:
Arlene, the word
drawn out into a plea,
and yet a joy
from somewhere
in your heart.

I came toward you
with Liza, your fourth
grandchild, at my side.

She wheeled you,
and you seemed at peace,
the shadows of your mind
bathed in a light for now.
I'd never felt so loved
as when your fading memory
was filled with me.

"So *you're* Arlene,"
the nurse had said
with feeling.
I do exist, I thought.

ANOTHER POINT OF VIEW

(For Father)

"Dat's anudder pernt of view,
 Dat's anudder pernt of view,
 Dat's anudder pernt,
 Anudder pernt of view."

I mimicked you, that Lower East Side
accent that I took for granted.

I can't remember the context
of that song we sang together
like a vaudeville team, pointing
fingers at each other in mock
chastisement or just plain
silliness.

I can't remember what it was
that led us to that singing,
but honestly, I never heard
about another point of view
except from you,

and it just never registered,
because you sang yourself
with me but never said
a serious thing: you left it

up to *her* to say things that
would indicate she couldn't
see another point of view,

and when I had to pick a way to be
that wasn't her but might be me
enough to last till now,
I made my slogans out of songs,
our songs, and couldn't know
the limitations on them, like
the way one point of view
is right for you one time
and not another.

By the time I might have asked
about all that, you'd
disappeared into your work,
as if an amputation had been
done on us, and I have spent
my life in excess of belief
that always, always, there's
another point of view,
in search, dear Father,
of the likes of you.

REFLECTIONS

Walking in the woods
I say I've finally returned
to that same place where
I once dreamed of what I've
come to be,

and here are all the acorns,
the path that circles to the
lake. The leafless trees
make etchings on the sky. It
is the same but not the same:

Each thing has its familiar
name but is not that *exact*
thing that I need to find,
and you and everything are
not familiar entities, but
circumstantial evidence of
these, my name-tagged
longings.

It's here I need to rest,
to ponder how to keep this
woods, to be a child absorbed
in nothing more than pocketing
my share of acorns. Call

them "something I was fond
of"—acorns, woods, that path
that circles to the lake,

like "living" circles to a close,
and "living things" evolve to
something other than they were,
and "coming back" can never be
the same.

OUR HOUSE

Yesterday, while walking near the sea,
I passed a house like ours,
the one we sold but never left
ten years ago.

I almost lost myself in longing
for our wide gray porch,
our front door's beveled glass,
bow windows to the left and right.
I wanted so much to be back inside,
to welcome myself in.

I knew that house as if
we'd lived there all this time:
the piano in the front hall alcove,
and above, the staircase
paneled in fine wood
and curving gracefully,
while straight ahead along the corridor
our kitchen, hardly modern
but so adequate.

I half expected, from my point of view
outside and thinking in,
to see the children tumbling out
in pairs, perhaps, not really

seeing me, a stranger, but aware,
I hoped, of some warm feeling
on my part.

I could go on this way,
but we both know that
nothing stays the same—
not you, nor I, nor children;
everything is in its place,
but somewhere else.

And now it's condominiums,
bits of busy work for us,
emails, phone calls,
and infrequent visits
while waiting for the past
to come along and rescue us
in time.

ESTES PARK

(For Cara)

Even in Estes Park the stubble grows,
there upon the uppermost plateaus,
where ancient rock of Colorado's range
is barest to the sun.

How terribly strange to climb your way
up there, only to find that you've not
left your scratchy thorns behind
in daring to allow yourself that height.

We slept in Estes Park that summer night,
a treat, they said, to mark my visit there
in Boulder. My girl wore flowers
in her hair and leaned her head
upon her lover's arm so tenderly.

Could there be any harm in being part
of youth's idyllic fling? I'd been invited;
that said everything of where
the young ones were and where I stood,
away from judgment-making, bad or good,
right or wrong, or something in between,
up there in Estes Park.
That's what I mean by saying that
in highest places grow the wildest things

that we can ever know, such things of beauty,
and of plainness, too, equally poised and
open to God's view, so far removed from
those who would assess a moral value,
moral worthiness.

We'd had to come to Estes Park to see
how whole we could become. How true.
    How free.

ROOMS

I have had as many children
as this house has rooms,
and when the rooms have grown
sullen and worn, I have pasted
new wallpaper, cleaned the
rugs, and changed to more
dependable colors.

But when the children have
changed to sullen, they have
left their rooms to my care,
have left me sullen and worn.

I have explained that a
touch-up with brighter hues
was entirely possible in my
case, to be as good as new.

They have said, but not in
unison: *It is not possible.*
The cost of such repair is
too dear. We will find new,
brighter places. But be
patient. We will from time
to time brighten things
here and there.

I had no choice but to polish
the facade from day to day.
When that went, the repairs
became unmanageable and so
I redecorated in my own time,
with my own taste, and now
the decor is, at last,
eclectic, like myself.

RECOVERY

At twenty-six you count
impediments like black
nail holes in newly
painted walls,

speaking of judgment lapses,
Past ambivalence, you lean
upon your pillow like a child
upon a sickbed: the pillow's
sag exactly fits the head
it cradles.

Reports of medical recovery
laud early ambulation in post-
surgery, the cutting and
suturing over with.

Now it's out of bed you go,
weak in the knees but aiming
straightway for the door,
unsteady along the corridor
into the flow of ambulatory
others.
Steady, girl. Now, here's
a hand, in case you haven't
noticed; lean a bit. It's

customary: we have been this
way before.

ROCKAWAY ONE

There was no elegance
about the boarding house:
a matter of two floors
of rooms, each with a sink,
no bath (there was one
in the hall), a balcony
(each room has one) where
sometimes, as a rule, on
those Sundays when the
husbands were in residence,
politics and temperaments
might clash.

My father, long a Democrat,
had no damned use for Dr.
Cohn, the dentist, called
him dirty bastard Communist,
and threatened him with
upraised fist as bantam
Dr. Cohn leaned on his
railing shaking somewhat
smaller fists and saying:
*Ida, let me go, he's
starting in again!*

Father, always ready to

do battle with opposing
viewpoints, would glare down
at Dr. Cohn and poise himself
to vault our railing to
confront that *Commie Cohn*,
but instead might spit a wad
across at him in spite of
Mother's protest, shouting: *Bess,
the guy's a bastard COMMUNIST!*

That the boarding house
was well aware of, having
heard it all before: In 1945
it was the thing to do,
that being firmly Democrat,
and not so popular a thing,
that being Communist.

And when the two of them
quit brawling, hissing,
spitting, stamping, things
would quiet down. Later, in
the dining room, the Cohns
and Joffes ate on oilcloth
at their separate tables.

It was not discussed, but
judging by the missuses on
Monday mornings,sharing
nice warm conversations

in the common kitchen, no
harm done, and if the men
were wont to scratch each
other's eyes out every
Sunday over trivialities,
well . . . what could you
do . . .

ROCKAWAY TWO

We used to wait on clear days,
eyes glued to the watery horizon.
There it is! we'd shout. *A ship!*

It could have been a barge,
or someone's pleasure boat,
but what we *wanted* it to be,
our feet glued to the shore,
was some great ocean liner
bound from somewhere
in a horizontal line
from where we stood.

We didn't mark the distance,
understand the parallel,
but thought how marvelous it felt
to know its path and ours could cross.

Later, after Rockaway,
we were to measure distance
carefully and learn that
some things running parallel
maintain a distance, can't
be thrown off course, and
since it didn't matter,
let it be,

while other things, like love
and so on, veer so suddenly
off course, and that depends
on tow and knowing when to
slack the line or draw it in.

ROCKAWAY THREE

When the ocean threw a crab,
half eaten, legs half severed,
on the sand, it never was
the same for him:

Now no array of pink-lined
shells, black seaweed good for
popping, or the tiny pebbles
meant to fortify his castles,
makes it safe.

His steps down from
the boardwalk, through the
white-hot sand to where it
darkens at the ocean's rim
are planned with care, made
wary, knowing death
can happen here, can
happen anywhere.

ROCKAWAY FOUR

Along the boardwalk,
two miles down past our
street, past Curley's
Baths, the first-aid
station, and the stores
where summer people
shopped, past 116th
Street, where the LIRR
spilled our fathers
out on Fridays, scooped
them up on Mondays,

somewhere past Belle
Harbor, where the
rich folks stayed,
just glad to get away
from crowded city streets.
Past St. Mary's
convent, but before
you came to Playland
with its monster of
a steeplechase, the
largest in the world
back then,
somewhere in between
stays in my memory:

the only place I'd stop
along my route to lean
against the silver
boardwalk rail and
watch the children of
the Crippled Orphans'
Home get wheeled across
the ramp that brought
them to the sand, where
white-garbed aides
arranged them in a
circle in between the
water and the steps.

Their faces are a
blur to me, but not
their legs, unworkable
and hanging down or
strapped to perpendicular.

Do they care? I wondered,
for their faces did not
indicate a preference.
I could not stay to see
what my two working
limbs might mean to them.
It mattered somehow.
And how short the trip
returning seemed to be,
My two brown legs

gallumping with a spring
miraculous.

It takes a sight like
that to make you look
at what you've got:
two legs that work like
pistons running down
the boardwalk steps,
across the hot sand,
feeling it acutely,
feeling then the cooler,
browner sand and then
the cold, cold water,

stepping over tangled
seaweed, broken shells,
the bottom's textured,
sucking-in grave mystery
that some of us (not all,
I was aware)are free
to know.

ROCKAWAY FIVE

Romelia and Joe were
oddities those summers,
walking hand in hand,
her brown, sun-seasoned
fingers, ruby-polished
nails, her diamond band
third finger left, while
on his sunburned hand a
moonstone set in platinum
fifth finger right.

Their daily walks together
had a never-changing
pattern: brisk pace in
tandem, breaking stride
to wave, but nothing more.
Each morning when the sun
was on its way to scorching
height, they two left other
early birds to wonder into
what horizon they were headed.

This was not mentioned in
the evenings when, still
hand in hand, but much
more leisurely, they

strolled the lamp-lit
boardwalk and, conforming
to a social ritual,
stopped and moved apart, he
to join the men whose
cigarettes, cigars bespoke
of leisure class, while she
and other wives would fall
behind their men or walk ahead,
speaking through red bow-lips,
white snoods perched upon
their marcelled hair, their
fingers ringed in diamonds
or, in Romy's case, large
emeralds.

Oh, it was elegant and
beautiful, that summer life
of theirs, the love that
no one, to my knowledge,
mused about—or mocked, as
might have been the case
with many, though in
retrospect, it certainly
deserved their envy, if
they understood at all.
Romelia and her Joe
have long passed on,
leaving us to dream we
see them strolling side

by side somewhere beyond
the eyes of those of us
who spent our summers on
the beaches and the board-
walk, looking out across
the ocean and the sand.

ROCKAWAY SIX

The women in their skirted
bathing suits stand side by
side along the rope, like
plump and bobbing beads,
dipping and weaving, falling
back against each other when
the great waves come,
determination in their eyes,
and yet, the bow-lipped smile
to indicate their pleasure—
or their triumph over fear.

It is a simple matter
that the men, made to go
out beyond the crashing
waves by protocol, give
little thought to women
things: the act of
giving birth and
doing it despite the pain,
and all the rest that is
ordained but not devoid
of risk.
They, their women,
never think of floating
out beyond the breakers,

knowing how it would
be viewed:

She takes such chances
with her life, which isn't
hers to risk. What of the
babies who depend on her?

Women hold the rope,
and if they fall, their
bosoms and their thighs
are cushions for each
other's life,

and they come bobbing up
like gem-beads
set in steel.

NOTHING

Nothing moves me to despair,
not rain or clouds when I expected sun,
not loss of superficial things
that were not meant to last at all
and were not given as a birthright.

I say, *Nothing moves me to despair.*
I say that after living through debacles
of a major sort.

Living them, I said,
you will look back to see
that you have come to say
that nothing moves you to despair.
And you will say that too.

Yet all that I have said, and say,
is all *my* truth, and all
that is reliable for *me.*

Saying *Nothing moves me to despair,*
though self-deceiving is, of course,
untrue, but comforts me, and so
I share the ruse, in hopes that
it can do the same for you.

RAGMAN

The ragman
comes collecting.

I admit him, press my
olive brown skin, heavy
lidded eyes against
the brown cloth rags
of him.

There is the smell of
childhood, of the
cabbage boiling on
the baked enamel stove,
clothes hung on drying
rack above my mother's
black curled hair,

father's thick cigars
and that peculiar old
skin smell of laps on
which I slept sometimes:
my older aunts.

The ragman's eyes do
penetrate the color
of my cheek, the

reddened lips, my mask
of garish rouge, emulsions
that dissemble from
this brown and heavy-
lidded *Mediterranee.*

The ragman
from the courtyard
of my tenement is
not now calling up to
dusty windows closed
against his *shofar*
wail.

*This is no time to
stand on ceremony,*
he says, eye on my
eye, *It is the time
for cashing clothes.*

RAGMAN TWO

I hear the footsteps of the ragman fall.
Oh, mama, the courtyard's cold and dark!
His fingers point to where I sit
clean-shaven.

Cash clothes! Cash clothes!
His voice croaks like a broken heart.
Oh mama, close my eyes to madness.
I shall write a sonnet to the hapless
poor.

The wind has blown the ragman's bundle
down and strewn its contents.
Mama, call to me, make pretense to
demand of me an ode to happiness, a
song so sweet that all that lies about
the ragman's feet is hidden from my eyes.

THE STAIN

The dark stain on the oriental rug
in that perfect living room
spoke of a kinder time.

"It was the dog," my mother said,
"The chow, Chin-Chin.
"We had to give him up
because of you."

No rancor there.
I warmed to her for that,
and took it for a sign
of possibility.

"Feet off the couch," she said
in that peculiar way,
her eyes black holes again,
the twinkle gone much like
a space left by a falling star.

The rug stain mocked me
with its permanence.

ESCAPE

You *look* like me
but hardly want to
be like me,
floating off to
California, Utah,
wanting mountains,
bicycle paths,
slopes for sliding,
surf for lifting
some genetic burdens.

You once said that
I envied you.
I do. Stuck here,
I go a different
path, wanting to
look like *someone*
whose womb held me
long enough to drop
the girl bundle, *me*,
in the Bronx of nineteen
thirty-one.

Knowing who you are,
you know you are not
me, but *of* me. Knowing

I am someone but not
who exactly, I cannot
be *anyone* at all.

Knowing who I am to *you,*
could you take me with
you to the Mormon country
where the little town
you love is hidden?

Maybe you know *something*
spelled out in the genes,
from *her* to me to you.
Maybe you could lead me
out.

Whoever

GRASS

The season's growth of grass
is higher than the railing
of our summer place.

He cut it down last season
to a stubble height; yet,
here it is, full grown again.

It seems unfair.

Things rise again–
the grass, the bulbs–
in season's time,
but he is gone and planted
in another place somewhere.

It's left to Bob or Bill,
his boys, to tend the grass,
which they will do
when cutting down
means *things* again.

OLD AGE OF A HARRIDAN

When silence falls,
a scream rings hollow
as her memory sends it
up to present time,

But falling short of
its dyspeptic mark,
it threads out from her
throat,

Between clenched
teeth and through lips
tight with customary
rage,

To make a mewing
sound whose syllables—
benign, forgiving—
approximate

I
  Hate
    You

MISS LYDIA

In Miss Lydia's present,
the ground is curved and rutted,
songs are louder, their words
muffled, hum of the fan is
someone back there playing
an impromptu concert.

Earth has surely moved,
for heat is hotter, cold
more penetrating.

She, the Orwell of her time,
but almost empty of
predictions now,
has only one.

KATE

Catching a glimpse of Kate
watch two persistent sea
gulls begging food, we see
a comprehension not afforded
her by what *we* have to say:

She has a way of listening,
lips pursed to sour, for a
long-expected slight,
then issuing her verbal
self-defense with venom
carried on saliva spray.

Then Kate retracts her tongue
and turns her beach chair
back to us, bag of bread
crumbs poised to feed her
tender mercy to the birds.

WALL

At sixty-five he built a wall,
I mean, quite literally, *a wall*
of stones, that kind of wall
that takes the gathering of
stones, the mixing of cement,
the laying out those stones
to form a monument, that is,
a wall not meant for coming through,
but meant as barrier for strangers,
telling them they must not enter
there.

In time, he knew, a stranger
would appear, to glide beyond the
wall as no mere mortal could,
and lead him out the door,
past the swing set he'd once built
for babies long since gone,
and past the pergola he'd fashioned
for his wife with love, then
finally across the wall of stones
to where those strangers used to
stand and watch so longingly, so
full of curiosity.

The thought of it, that last

scenario, made him frantic to complete the wall, to find the stones and mix the concrete by himself to get it done in time. *His* time.

RAIN

Sheets of windswept rain,
torrents from black-clouded
heavens, fall like blows
from some predictive force
upon her shoulders. So it
seems to her, frail, very old,
with bones that, having
once framed youthful
roundness, now have given up
the task assigned to them,
serving as warning to her
still-clear mind of dreadful
things to come . . .
like death . . .

And bones and rain conspire
now to make a gloom that
cuts her to the heart
and translates into pain
and ache, stiffness and
a certain lassitude that
is considered common
in the Old.
Seated on her kitchen chair,
she has an oblique view of sky,
the tops of trees, the roof

of house next door. No comfort
there, when comfort is the all
of what her age must have to
slow the steady pace of death.

When evening comes, we face
her, fresh from our day's work,
and, satisfied, ask in absent-
minded tones how her day went,
shamelessly annoyed when the
reply—so flat, so sad, so
pleading—takes away our peace:
    It hurts. You know
    the rain's no good for me.

At that a grimace to connect
her pain with us, for solace
if for nothing else. But seeing
what effect her words have
on our tiredness, she sinks back
into anonymity, giving us
the gift of taking back her
words, her pain, and leaving us
our youth:
    I guess the trees need rain,
    and then tomorrow I'll be
    more myself.

And we, turned blind, accept her
words as truth.

RACHEL MONDAY

Rachel Monday rose from the kitchen
table, rather slithered along its length,
staring down all the while at
the crumpled figure of her mother.

Rachel was filled with no pity,
no abhorrence of the matted hair
that clung to Mother's sallow
cheeks covered with the
viscous liquid planned to be
the dinner's soup.

Always the same way it would
happen, in that yellow kitchen
with its ruffled curtains
of white dotted swiss against
the blackness of the night,

right there where Mother's
plants grew tall and healthy,
bathed in sunshine
through the quiet afternoons
when Mother sat at that same
table mending, stood
at the stove where stew was
simmering, watching it

as if it bore some great
importance beyond
a dinner's fare,

standing at the window
looking down at cars, the steep
hill almost vertical,
that ended at the park—
doing nothing really,

but with such a sense
of order, such solitary peace,
it seemed to Rachel that
the days and nights of Rachel's
childhood had an aura of
predictability.

Except for that, that dinner time
more often than she wanted to
acknowledge, or maybe in spite of,
or even *because* of that, the *shock*,
like water thrown against a pane
of glass—because of *that* the rest
seemed almost eery in its
silence.

When it began she knew the sequence
of events to come: the sudden rage,
the food spat out from Father's gaping
mouth, the bowl of soup he'd lift high

overhead, then, cursing, smash it
down. Down where? On Mother's
head.

But had he meant it just that way?
Suppose he'd meant to fling the
bowl across or down or anywhere,
but somehow, in a cruel and un-
intentioned quirk of time awry,
she had collided with it. There
she lay, the question of
intent no longer relevant.

In the yellow-painted kitchen
with its spotless porcelain sink,
its black-knobbed stove, its ruffled
curtains, the tall and graceful
plants in red-and-blue ceramic pots,
white iridescent canisters of china,
and the yellow breadbox—around the table
where the three of them ate silently
at night, violence occurred.

Mother lay curled like a child, not
moving, but moaning softly, like a
fawn run over in a sudden crush of
violent encounter. Rachel, like that
wounded fawn, stood stunned and
motionless, staring down but helpless
to react.

When she left the kitchen, with
her mother lying on the polished
floor, a weariness came over her.
The dark, unlighted corridor, her
groping through it to her tulip-
papered room, the comfort of
the covers, the safe, still stifling of
her rage and shame beneath the quilt,
were images of such nights too vivid
to erase.

Later, having slept away the terror,
she would recognize her mother's
footsteps, wait, expect her door to open
as it always did, revealing Mother's
tired form. *Come on, get up and say
you're sorry, Rachel. Tell your father that.*
She always did, for reasons not her own.

She'd say her sorries, but the form upon
the bed did not acknowledge that he'd heard.
It didn't matter. What *did* matter was her
mother's kneeling by his side, patting his
hand, which dangled down in evident ennui,
patting the stolid, sullen cheek that never
turned toward her, pleading *Please, she's
said she's sorry. See, she's said it.*

A softening came over Father's face, and

it was time for Rachel to leave the two
alone, go back into the flowered room
no wiser than before but somehow safer,
with the violence left outside and only
embryos of terror on her bedroom wall.

TULIPS TWO

A life ago
I stared at tulips
on my wall, grew
tired of their
symmetry that
clashed with how
my life was
shaping up,

said to the tulips
with mock levity,
"Stay there. I will
catch up with you."

In twenty years
I filled four rooms
with tulips that
had sprung to life
defying symmetry.

It was, I tell you,
an accomplishment.

In twenty more
the tulips found
the soil best

suited to their style.

It was, I tell you,
an accomplishment to
get them off my wall
and out of symmetry.

But God! How blank
the wall has gotten
since the tulips
        bloomed.

MARGIE

When I find my cousin Margie,
Daddy's sister's girl,
I will remind her of our
Sunday visits, how we sat
on top of clothes piled on
her bed and she would tell
me of her crush on Mrs. Laver,
who had taught her
French at Hunter, and how
she, with all her troubles,
took the time to teach me
Latin vowels, and how
she plied me full of
candies, though I knew she
could not stand the sight
of me, which I could
understand, she being in
that dark apartment at
the residence hotel where
Jim, her father, Doctor Jim,
was slowly dying of leukemia
through all those years we
were in college.
I will mention that I did
not know my father'd
helped her family out with

food and rent (It was
Depression days back then
and doctors like my Uncle
Jim were barely making it)
and that, if tables had
been turned, I would have
hated Margie too.

I will tell her how I
felt when she came down
with what they call Bell's
Palsy and it made her face
go up on one side, down
the other, and how treatment
didn't help,

and how the acne scars just
added to the mess and I did
pity her, but I *did* think
her rhinoplasty was a great
success.

I often wonder how, through
all these years, I haven't
heard from her except to know
she changed her name and moved
away from everyone.

Now sixty years have passed
and still I wonder why

she hasn't kept
in touch.

SOME

(East Bronx, 1930s)

They were poor in walk-up
tenements whose stairs and
halls smelled cabbage,
chicken soup,

and in their kitchen water
boiled away, and hands
with raw and reddened
flesh stirred bits of
anything inside the pot
while too-small wide gold
wedding bands cut deep into
the work-worn flesh.

Across the street, in the
near-new apartment building
where her people lived,
the tenants were not poor, the
ladies clothed in gowns
with beaded bands across
their marcelled hair, their
powdered foreheads, charcoaled
eyes and painted bow lips
made suggestive by design.

Her father's chums wore
suits with vests, the pockets
filled with good cigars, and
from their waists hung watches
made of gold, the cases scrolled
and monogrammed,

Often, from her bedroom window,
she would watch the tenements,
their shades askew, revealing
men in sleeveless undershirts
and women bending in and out
of dreary tasks.

She would watch them from
her bedroom window framed
in eyelet, the carpet made of
colored squares in rich and
muted tones, with velour-papered walls
hung with imported
art.

From the silence of that
velour-papered room she'd
lean against her curtained glass
to watch the shadows move
across the shades, and mark
the rituals of family life
until she knew them all by
heart: the mother at the

stove, the father walking
through the windowed rooms,
the children running back
and forth across the window
view, and all of them together
framing, in her mind, a
family.

In her heart she'd float
beyond the barriers of glass,
beyond the boundaries of
silence and across the narrow
street that separated her
from her fair portion of their
tender family life, calling
them by names that were,
she wished, her own.

DINNER AT CHARLIE'S

Charlie is approachable
just on the other side
of controversy,

on an island just across
white linen tablecloth,
roast lamb, and steaming
vegetables,

terrain to obfuscate
the view from where
you sit to where he
stands politically.

The tea and scones,
the clotted cream, the
scent of jasmine swirling

round the barbs and thrusts
that spice the conversation
held primarily between
Charlie and himself

hardly make for something
homogeneous, but give,
despite the hospitality

intended by the host,
a gastronomic jolt.

The time for *au revoir*
has come. You . . . hate . . .
To leave, and know that
Charlie hates . . . to see
you go.

He, being not quite
done with his soliloquy,
his dinner discourse,

hungers for a bite of *you*,
a sliver of your mincemeat
pie, of mincemeat in
particular.

You, without an appetite for it,
think how you're really
finished this time,
solidly fed up.

You offer your limp hand,
your left cheek,
which he kisses
vacantly.

He seems exhausted,
like a lion after

dining on some
sumptuous repast.

At last, at last,
your eyes not meeting
his, and thinking
of the spider and
the fly,

you sidle by him,
make your fisted hand
behave in semblance
of a wave.
Goodbye.

MARY ROSE

Mary Rose, her walker
and her mother's needlepoints,
belonged to Richard
and his wife and son,
like an old and once-loved pet
that one has made a promise to,
and is by conscience
bound to keep to it.

Mary Rose need not have left
her life in Richard's hand,
but with no inner vision
of a different path to take,
willed on herself that role.

It was so understandable,
that stripping bare of
purpose and proclivity:
to be disabled, and a widow,
may leave one without the
former steel that would have
risen over burning coals
and persevered.
Once, Mary Rose had that,
but death had come too close
to be outdistanced,

and the numbness settled in,
a waiting that required
only iron will.

There were no tears,
no longings, to be seen
in Mary Rose. Moving
as they moved, accommodating
to their changes,
Mary Rose sat still.

In time, the air grew smoky,
voices thinned to where they
grew unrecognizable.
Cold slipped in the house
that seemed to have grown
longer, darker, ghostlike.
Mary Rose sat still.
Food was presented,
guest came and departed,
children once adored by
her arrived, then left,
strangers came with questions
that she answered willingly
as best she could, all
sense of danger gone
with muscles, cells and bone.
And Mary Rose sat still.

Those that willed her

docile were now not so sure
of what they felt or thought,
and wished that Mary Rose,
the old, vain, feisty one
who wouldn't have allowed
herself to sit stock still,
would rise in fury one more
time or else the battle
was unfair,

while Mary Rose, deep down,
by habit and recalcitrance,
leaned back against her
yellow satin chair, seemed
to be nodding off, and,
having once again defeated
them, sat, still.

OLD GUY

He hears the traffic
on the highway just beyond the house
and wonders why it never bothered him
before in just this way.

She knows that once he too
was part of it, that moving
in tandem with the others
going purposely from
here to there and back again.

Now he sees that newer models
are in transit, with younger
faces at the wheels,
and just as he was once,
the highway bunch are much too
busy thinking of the jobs
ahead of them to wonder
what that old guy sitting
in his house has up his sleeve,

while she sees something
in his eyes, a cross between
despair and puzzlement.

She doesn't hear the traffic

half as much and wonders
if she's gotten deaf
or whether he is dreaming,

and does it matter
  in the short run
    after all?

THE CAPTAIN'S DAUGHTER

The captain's daughter
Comes to where he sits,
Land-locked at last.

"I'm glad you're here," she says.
    I've needed you."

But he, used to the sea,
Where something either
Sinks or swims,
But never both,
Looks at his daughter,
Grown out of some wild pain,
Now whole again,

And wonders how it came to be
That she has neither sunk
Nor swum consistently,
And how, although her ship
Has run off course,
She has not perished.

Nothing he has ever seen or known
Can quite compare:
Water is water, air is air.
Yet she, no captain,

And without a sextant,
Buried by sea foam,
In spite of all
Has made the voyage home.

MUJERES

The women come by bus,
read their bibles
while *they are prepared.*
  Señor Jesus . . . Benedicion.
  Señor Jesus . . . Gracias.

Their voices lament forth
their trust, their adoration:
Doctor Blanco, Medicaid, their *santos.*

Doctor's eyes dart past their own.
  "Dolor?" The word floats overhead.
  "No mucho," they reply respectfully,
language not a common bond between them.

When the surgery is done, the tubes
removed, and they have borne the pain,
the women brush their hair back
from their smooth brown temples,

change from the issued gowns
into their flowered sweaters
and blue jeans, then take the
crosstown bus back home.

Whatever

DON'T COUNT YOUR CHICKENS

"Don't count your chickens
'Fore they hatch."
I didn't.

Now I've got a batch:
More than four
But less'n a dozen,
All squawkin', cluckin',
Scratchin', buzzin'.

Some of 'em are in there struttin'.
Some of 'em are doin' nuttin'
But pushin' the others outta the nest,
Wantin' to be judged the best.

Boy, I'd like to see the day
When some game cocks steal 'em away,
Give 'em chickies of their own,
And finally leave me alone!

PASTA FA YOU

With a bowl of thin spaghetti
  Balanced neatly in her palm
She regarded the intruder
  With a superficial calm.

"Just don't move and I won't hurt you,"
  He said, whipping out a gun.
She begged in a Spanish accent,
  "Let me get the cinnamon."

"I will have to burn the house down
  If you don't show me the loot!"
"Just a little Sweet & Low," she said.
  "It's in my husband's suit."

"You're a cuckoo," he said hotly.
  "Put that lousy stuff away!"
"If you let me eat my pasta
  I'll do anything you say."

"Forget about dat pasta!"
  That was all the fellow'd said,
When she threw the bowl of pasta,
  Which then struck him on the head.
As it landed full face forward
  She observed with great surprise

How the tasty glob of pasta
  Stuck around his nose and eyes.

"Now you've ruined my favorite dinner!"
  That was all that she had said,
When he staggered and he sputtered
  And then hit the floor, quite dead.

She explained to the detective
  It had been her only wish
To enjoy her bowl of pasta,
  As it was her favorite dish.

"What was in that dish of pasta?"
  "Oh, some cinnamon. . .Sweet & Low."
The detective muttered sadly,
  "What an awful way to go.

"We could send you up for murder,
  Or manslaughter with *intente*.
It is obvious your weapon
  Was that lethal pasta *al dente!*"

"I confess; put me in prison,
  But make sure that it is one
That puts in a good supply of
  Sweet & Low and cinnamon."

TIBET

The imperial palace
  In ancient Tibet
Was in turmoil, the Lama
  Extremely upset
By the news that, outside
  Of his own sacred walls
Construction had started
  On three mini-malls,
Two luxury condos,
  An airport as well;
And to top it all off
  There was planned a hotel
Where a clever tour mogul
  Named Manny Petrillo
Planned to house rich vacationers
  Seeking a thrill.
Oh, and what could they do
  With that Western barbarian
Whose billboard signs read,
  "Tibet Homes by Azarian"?

The lama stared out of
  His seven-foot moat,
Trying to swallow
  The lump in his throat.
"Our mountain paths soon

Shall become great impasses
  As the Western hordes come
Climbing up on their asses."
  He called into conclave
His most pious monks,
  And there they all sat
In the deepest of funks.
  "This is the place that they've
All had their eyes on
  Since damned fools in Hollywood
Made 'Lost Horizon.'"
  There seemed no way out of it;
Plans were all set
  For the Madison Avenue coup of Tibet!

Though Tibetans had never
  Been known as mercurial,
There emerged from their ranks
  Some more entrepreneurial
Who, fresh from the states
  With their new MBAs
Quoted "Anything goes,
  Just as long as it pays."
They said to their Lama,
  "Come down from your aerie;
There's no time for dalliance."
  Their voices were fiery
And rung with such truth that
  The monks left their orders
And welcomed the Westerners

Into their borders
With signs reading, "Home of
  The Dalai High Lama,
The best place to find your
  Particular karma.
In Shangri-la prices
  Are always sky-high,
But it's one place on Earth
  Where your business won't die!"

FINDING GOD

I bought some God at a convenience store,
And took a swig behind the fast food aisle,
And paid for it with pocketfuls of change,
And gave the clerk a radiating smile.

In the car I tilted down the seat
And drank the rest in deep and thirsty drafts,
The way Titanic's courtly passengers,
Run out of lifeboats, dashed for flimsy rafts.

That God, I thought, *is really potent stuff!*
As long-lost courage filled my heavy heart.
I made another trip to that same store
And finding God, filled up my shopping cart.

Three people were ahead of me in line,
And two of them, I saw, had found God, too.
"We wouldn't be without it," they agreed.
"And it's available in capsules too!"

Last week I came back to the neighborhood
And stepped into that old convenience store,
Went down the aisle but couldn't find the God,
And learned they didn't stock it anymore.
"But we've got something new," the clerk announced,
"And you can buy a six-pack if you wanna."

I took him at his word and tried it out,
And now I'm glad to say I've found Nirvana.

METAMORPHOSIS

Once they called her all legs,
Later: all chest.
Finally: all thumbs.
Not yet: a bag of wind.

But let's not hold our breath.

THE PATRIOT

T'was told in legend years gone by,
Of the man who bit the tsetse fly.
When town criers spread the news,
It drove away the people's blues.
It raised their hackles too, of course:
A myth gone dry is no small loss.

It seems this fellow made a trip
To Africa, and got a grip
On one large specie pointed out
By some old shaman thereabout
Who claimed–although his facts were vague–
That such a one had caused the plague!

Without so much as *by your leave*,
This altruist rolled up his sleeve,
And with a sharp turn of his wrist
Caught the tsetse in his fist!
Now, this is what the legend said:
He then bit off the tsetse's head!

His actions caused a brouhaha.
"You have, dear fellow, gone too far.
You've killed without the right to do it.
And then to boast there's nothing to it!
Reports on the supposed plague

Are, on the whole, extremely vague."

All sorts of groups involved with rights
Became embroiled in bitter fights
With epidemiologists
Who crossed the tsetse off their lists
Of plaguers of the human race.
It was a pretty nasty case.

A gross injustice, it was said,
To crassly kill a creature dead
Because it had been thought to be
The cause of a catastrophe.
The banners waved for all to see:
SAVE THE INNOCENT TSETSE!

The press, as is its wont in matters
Controversial, tore to tatters
The poor man's credibility,
Claiming incivility,
While major universities
Reacted to divers degrees.

Home the killer came to censure,
To threats against his lethal denture,
Hanging him in effigy.
How dare he harm the poor tsetse!
His claim of national defense
Was deemed a lack of common sense.

Written off as a disgrace
To both his country and his race,
He, who'd bit with best intention,
Was stripped of title and of pension.
Eventually, the poor soul died,
Having swallowed the tsetse and his pride.

Whenever

HERE ARE ALL THE ACORNS

Walking in the woods,
I say I've finally returned
  to that same place
  where I once dreamed of
  what I've come to be.

Ah, here are all the acorns,
the path that circles to the lake,
  the leafless trees like etchings
  on the sky. It is the same
  but not the same:

Each thing has its familiar name
but is not that *exact* thing
  that I need to find,
  and you and I and everything
  are not familiar entities,
  but circumstantial evidence
  of these old name-tagged
  longings.

It's here I need to rest,
to ponder how to keep this woods,
  to be a child again, absorbed
  in nothing more than pocketing
  my share of acorns.

Call them *something I was fond of*:
acorns, woods, that winding path
  that circles to the lake,
  like living always circles
  to a close, and living things
  evolve to something other
  than they were, and coming back
  is yet another truth.

MELTDOWN

Trying to get by you
when we're sliding on
a patch of tacks—
well, there's no
satisfaction
in it:

and besides,
like Beelzebub
taken aback by
some formidable
extended cross,

your hand, with sparks
of light reflected from
your wedding band, that
tender and exonerating
shield. . .

well, the sparks
melt down the tacks.
And that was your intention,
wasn't it?

And all that dark
potential moves into

another room whose aura
we may vaguely feel

but one in which
we do not choose to go.

THERE IS A COST

Illusion peels away
in layers over time,
the climate having changed
from hot to cold:

Whatever to your eyes was
pleasant once now
seems inane.

Giving it a name, you call it
something being old that once
could capture puffs of
scented air, and it was
good . . .

Now, there,
don't come to the conclusion
that reality is something
less than warm and kind:

It is the mind that, marking
us superior (a fallacy), takes
flight, so that the nights
seem thrilling and the days
not chilling to the bone and
we don't notice just how

very much alone we are, how
little of our life we own

and how much promise our illusions
hold--and when they peel away in
shriveled strands we call it
being old and worse and something gone and
how can we go on . . .

And now our work is understanding
how to safely leave behind the
word-dreams of the past: Dreams,
by nature, can't be counted out
as ledger entries marking past
Account Receivables now fallen
into bankruptcies.

But then, come look at me.
Don't spare your scrutiny:
There is, you know, a thing
that felt like being there,
and now is not. You see it
in my eyes, and yours reflect
the same chagrin:

Having once chalked in a dream,
we can't erase it, but must mourn
its loss.

For each illusion gone there is

a price to pay, of course,
as life goes on.

THINGS TURN TO GUM

Things turn,
become sticky,
as untenable
as old gum,

and you just can't
take it anymore.
Makes you so sore
to see how things
get bitter that
were once so sweet,

so hard to chew on,
when there was a time
that you could swallow
anything

TAKING THE HEAT

The heat's a woolen blanket
folded tight, impossible to
peel. It will not give.

Clearing my throat,
I think that something
must be very wrong.
My heart? My lungs?

Or is it anger welling up?
Anger at what? I ask myself,
then cancel out the thought.

Too hot for anger. Just too hot,
I tell myself. *I thought you
learned to take the heat!*

THAT CERTAIN THREAD

Drawn into the web,
you bring your baggage
to that certain thread,
deposit it,
then put out your shingle:

RIPPLES

What am I entitled to? you ask,
as if you need to ask at all,
when you might rather ask
what *you* deserve according
to *your* lights, not mine, not
anyone's. For *I* in turn ask also
what *I* am entitled to of someone else.
And so it goes: one pebble
dropped into a pond, then
making twenty ripples soon
absorbed into the general flow,
ambiguous.

We are entitled to our time
on earth, no more, and what we make
of that depends on how we understand
biology.

My thoughts should be a comfort
somehow, lest your narcissistic bent
insists I answer questions that you
need to pose for some attention's sake.

How free you are when this bare
thought hits home.
How free I am of you.

EXTANT

When a thing exists
but isn't *this* or *that*,
do you believe it isn't
anything?

Or do you look at it
from out the corner
of your eye, as something
of a *shape* and, keeping it
a *fragment*, do you give
an explanation of it:
   Only *this* or *that*
   and *nothing really?*

Do you tiptoe by it,
hoping you are right—
that it has nothing that
you'd recognize as worthy
of a name, nor give a
good goddamn?

Then if that thing comes
up to you, looks you
in the eye, and says,
Do you know who I am?
Know what I am?

Would you then feel
you *could* not, *should* not,
would not be seen at that
thing's side?

And would you, bursting
with a certain kind
of pride, toss that *thing*,
that *gross anomaly*, that
unfamiliar *piece of life*
aside?

I would.

POINT OF VIEW

Tops of trees
are what I see best,
not striated barks
that clutch the earth,
or spindly branches
blown out blowsy
leafy green
for arboring
the leisure classes.

I do much better
with a window-framed
montage of bursting
foliage

from inside a room
made neon bright,
where books and papers,
business apparatuses,
bulky black and gray
facilitators of my
commerce stamped
with names like Canon,
Sharp and IBM,
share my space.

The view
from that perspective
is more stunning
and in harmony
with nature.
Mine, that is.

PRAYER

When time didn't matter
and age was ripe,
when all that mattered
was vast charm,
I counted good nature
above clarity of thought

But now that there's a squeeze,
give me a curmudgeon
who can keep the cerebral fluid
flowing.

Then, please God, let him
find some fault in me
and go on his way.

CIVILITY

Horns
 never honk
  at hearses
in deference
to a highway
that has no
 dividers,
  rest stops,
   U-turn
    designations,
    signs,
 The common exit
  understood

THERE ARE NO TRUMPETS

There are no trumpets.
Do not turn your ears away
from that plain-measured,
orderly andante stride
that, in your eyes, is not
enough.

There are no trumpets.
Yes, the violins and,
for a moment, here and
there in your decades,
horns of various degrees
and temperament.

But do not cock your ears
for trumpets: they do not
sustain, but can drown out
the orchestra,

until the beat, the essence
of the harmony you've made,
lost in the cacophony,
will fade.

THINGS

Once you have gone through
a thing, followed the thing
through, come out the other
door, and slammed it on the
thing, you think that one
more thing like that has
brought recovery.

Not so: You haven't
factored in the passing
of the years, the physical
economy, the tiredness,
the sense of how things
end and don't start up
again.

Not things.
Not clean recoveries.
Not anything.

LIVING LONG

Every day is not like
every other day:

The very ground we
stand on subtly shifts
beneath our feet,

and then our lungs
accommodate to new
demands placed on them
by a changing
atmosphere.

We have adjusted admirably
to what we are not forced
to see, while Time makes
each day seem more like
the last,

and now the challenge is
not *how* to live nor *if*
we can or will endure,

but what to *do* with
this long siege of time,
the vast terrain of it:

the deserts to traverse,
the rapids to maneuver
through with nothing but
bare hands,

and all the while the
mind, unfocused, and
bombarded with a million
choices, understands
the curse of so much
Time,

the living through
destruction, pain,
depression,
disappointment,
boredom,

and the likelihood
of tragedies, not once
but time and time again,
until we long for the
return of ignorance,
the expectation of an
end to one thing,
then the next,
and on and on,

till we start to want

to take control of Time
and make our own death
come within the proper
time frame: before
our children's and their
children's, and so forth
along the chain,

For if *that* changes,
too—if we become
survivors to our
children; if our aged
parents live, blind
and immobilized,
to see us buried;
if our roles are to
become as spiders
in a web, in which
we lie, the prisoners
of Time,

what does it matter
if that nature that
surrounds us behaves
subtly, or behaves
at all?
Let it explode
around us, make us
feel the chaos. Let
each day be unlike

every other in its
unpredictability,
so comfortable, so
philosophical,

and give us back
the definition
of *our* Time.

EMERGENCE

(As you find your way)

You say,
A *small thing has emerged*–
that is, a voice you own,
to your amazement.

What you mean—or *feel*–
for that's more like it,
knowing you—is that
the shrub you were that
has not seen a leaf or
bud in forty years
is now luxuriant,
but at a cost, of course,
that cost a loss of some
proportion.

Let's not speak of that
if we're to speak at all,
you warn, and knowing how
you think, I dare not push.
But, dear heart, something,
something has reamed out
the desiccated roots
that trapped your joy, and
now, no telling what you

will turn out to be.

Hopefully it will take on
a moderate costume and
leave some room for things
that mattered from the
bottom of the hole.

Just leave some room for me.

SEASONED

Come a little closer.
There is still time
to bond again. We are
still fond of one another.

See, the voices have died
down, the air is crisp and
silent. Days have mellowed,
narrowed to a path of leaves
and acorn shells.

Send our regrets: There's room
for only two to walk abreast.
The season's changed and we
are just in time.

ADVICE

They spoke their warnings,
telling her what she'd
regret, treading on her
readiness, cautioning
her, "Not yet."

Though she reminded them
of things gone bad,
it was beyond them then
to listen hard, their
minds closed down to
possibilities beyond
their ken.

That being true,
they set about their
task of answering for
her, as if she'd
even asked.

The years went by. Then,
when the need appeared
to have their say in
other matters unrelated
to the one before,
they couldn't bring

themselves to voice
their warnings in
the same old way,
and wondered why.

WEEPING-BED

Lifelong friendship's made in
weeping beds:

We cling together
in a bond of grief which, shared
for one brief moment in our time,
is dissipated, bringing sweet
relief.

That sorrow's milestone has been
set in stone, and with it,
friendship's solace and concern,

and even when, relieved of pain,
we rise from weeping bed and
dare to turn toward sun,

pursuing paths that nevermore
converge but separately turn
and twist instead,

we hold our common memory
undimmed, of friendship made
upon the weeping-bed.

WRONG

(Florida)

We had it all wrong,
thinking we could
make the day do anything.
A day, a week, a month
or two, or three.

If it rains we despair.
If the sun burns, we
complain, *What will we
do today? Where will we
go? What direction will
we take to pass the time.*

Next to us a pile
of books, a half-finished
afghan. Once it is dark,
there are the films,
the calls to make.

Did we forget a loved
one's birthday, a
promised phone call?
A gift to send?
Away from home, from
everything that keeps

us, there's the silence,
water flowing calmly,
birds perched on its banks.

Every word in every book
we've bought is read,
not skimmed, for here
there's sun, there's water;
here are palm trees.
Every single day

We do the little tasks
that make the day pass
while we, just the
two of us, remember
what it cost us,
in so many ways,
to come to Paradise,
and yet, ungratefully,
wait to go back home.

WHEN ONE BEAD BREAKS

When one bead of a
perfect necklace
breaks, the others
slide together to
present a picture
of perfection, where
nothing has been bent
out of the sequence
to the naked eye.

But lift the necklace
from its bed and see
how awkward the bare
string appears, and I,
in speaking for that
missing bead, insist
that necklaces form
gaps over the years,

and must be brought
to experts for repair—
that is, if she who
wore the necklace
proudly once
still cares.

CAGES

Cages
are benign
steel plaid
to which we
come with
purpose.

Not
ingenuously
we come
banging
on the bars,

shaking,
rattling
those bars
to be let in.

Let it be
said that's
so-and-so
in there,
and suddenly
that wild
lost creature
has a space

in which to
tack his name,

his nonexistence
ruptured into
neon spots
of notoriety,
witnessed better
through the bars
that concentrate
the image spread
for all to see.

We seek our cages
and incarcerate
ourselves within,

and curse
and rail
and throw
ourselves
against the
bars,

no longer
mute as when
we found
our cages
firmly
locked

against
ourselves
in flight.

FRAMES

I had a friend who thought
she'd fool time by changing
the sequence of everything
in her life, like cutting out
the backgrounds of snapshots,
cutting the snapshots to the
exact sizes of the faces,

taking all the faces and
gluing them next to, on top
of, near each other, taking
some of the cut-up scenery
and filling in the empty spots,
then putting the whole collage
into a handsome frame.

Is that your family? everyone
would ask, peering at the
dozens of young, older, much
older and much younger faces
that were smiling, frowning,
crying, reading, glaring—but
mostly smiling—at each other
or off to one side or out at
the viewer.
Yup. That's the family, all

of them, she would reply,
oblivious to the fact that
some faces appeared dozens of
times, some only once, and in
fact, some weren't there at
all. But that was the idea,
wasn't it?

We frame events so that they
show to best advantage. We
create our own poses for what
they say about our lives.
Wouldn't you agree? What can't
stand up to scrutiny can be cut
away, if it's snapshots we're
using to represent ourselves.

These are mine, we say, *This
is how they look, how they feel
about me, about each other.
This is how my past is welded to
my present. If you want to know
me, see the faces.*

How did you ever do it, the friends
of my friend would ask upon being
treated to a glimpse of the
family collage.
It wasn't easy but . . . she would
reply.

COMING OF AGE

Erotic love of self:
That is the comfort of old age—

Remembering
What may never have existed,
Entwining like and dislike,
Kindness and divisiveness,
Gentle touches, pummeling,
Humor and despair,
We use these to seduce ourselves.

Beyond eroticism,
We make passion of the past,
Feel exquisite pain
Of past mistakes,
The sensuous stroking
Of past compliments,
Keep mental autographs
Of suitors, friends,
Superiors long gone
Corporeally—and thus
So vivid in our memory.

We love more than we ever loved,
Racing to use up the words
Left in the bank from

Somewhere in the past,
When urgency was not the point.

It is, that certain flirting
With our memories,
The way we stroke the present,
Love ourselves to death.

NOTHINGNESS

Make time for Nothingness,
a state where products are intangible,
goals and deadlines mere semantics,
where the soil does not hold sorrow,

Where your ear hears silence
or the crickets chirping
in the woods at night.

Where your eyes accommodate to
light and shadow without
a sense of trepidation.

Let it all be as it will,
your heart more still than
when it bore its fill of
drama, every action
consequential.

Free of the tyranny imposed
by words, let silence
open all those long-embattled
senses.

Capture Nothingness again.

CIRCLING YOUR WAY HOME

Circling your way home,
you're bound to hit
some dead-end streets,
some highways closed,
MEN WORKING signs which you,
exhausted or preoccupied,
are tempted to ignore,
and therefore fall into
those manholes spite of
flashing lights and warning
flares, all that because you're
circling your way back,

unlike the time you took the highway
straight away from where you were
and landed in a heap along the way.

And so you use your map *this* time
at every turn, and plot the next,
giving thought to what terrain
you're bound to face,
and if you're up to it.

But roads were made
for going and returning;
each highway exit offers yet

another road along the way,
and that presents a challenge
to the mapping of your route.

Make a decision where to stop
and spend a night or two,
bypass construction,
take a scenic route,
and, coming down the pike,
know your direction,
noting all the signs that say
BEAR RIGHT
 SLOW DOWN
   FULL SPEED AHEAD
and get yourself
at your good speed
back home.

CHIMERA

Count yesterday as gone,
today but half a loaf,
tomorrow just a mystery.

There is no paper long enough
to re-create the days,
the years.

There is no memory
acute enough to store what was,
no eyes that focus long enough
on lessons learned.

There is no way
to let the truth come through
to where you *know* it's so,

to where you know
your truth has never,
does not *now*,
make sense.

CITY

When the night is awfully quiet
And the winds are dying down,
There's another world awakening
On the other side of town.

On the other side of cities
Where most folks are nestling in,
There's a game of chance in progress
In which nobody can win.

Oh, the old men flick their fingers
Over garments stiff with grime,
And they like to ask each other,
Mumbling softly, for the time.

Oh, the ladies sit demurely
In a corner with their things
Arranged neatly on the pavement,
Listening while a stranger sings.

Now and then there'll be a young one
Being charming for a taste
Of whatever's being offered.
In this world there is no waste.

Ah, see the stars a-glistening.

Smell the sultry air.
It's summer in the city,
As its people are aware.

Come on down, if you've a mind to,
And can leave your comfy bed.
It's a sight that must be seen
Before the players are all dead.

If you be an aunt or uncle,
Any kin to them, I say,
They have moved into the nighttime,
Leaving all of us the day.

Now, we know that all God's creatures
Have a purpose here on Earth,
So don't waste your time on pity
Or on reckoning their worth.

Keep on sleeping in your bedroom
Checkered up in pink and white,
Feel the comfort of the darkness
And the blindness of the night.

STEED

When I broke my steed,
I did not feel triumphant.
I did not feel I had won
the battle fairly, but
by attrition.

When I broke my steed
It obeyed too quickly,
moved too listlessly,
ate too nervously.

When I broke my steed
I broke its mold
and made it fit my own,

and both of us
became diminished.

ADOLESCENCE

Wanting everything came first,
expressed in howling, whining,
and, upon occasion,
honest tears.

Getting something, *anything*,
more than she had came next,
expressed in bucking the
establishment and hiding her
intent, producing the effect
of *growing up* at last.

Having lots of certain things,
Of certain everythings,
but certainly not of any
one thing was the reason
for new bitchiness, and
narrowed eyings of
contemporaries through a
prismed glass.

Understanding everything above
came late–not necessarily last—
appearing to be done with howling,
whining and more prone to honest tears.
And through at last, with

howlings, tantrums, and demanding
things, the surliness now
clearly seen as impotent,
she was, to them, more tractable,
but all that was, in her, still vital
and alive, though neatly underground,

She puffed her petulance,
was always on alert,
investigating possibilities
for a more certain future
in her field of expertise.

SHOW ME YOUR HANDS

(Reader of palms)

Show me your hands
and I will tell you what you were,
how you earned your living,
and maybe what you did
for other reasons.

Show me your hands
and I will tell you what you're like:
Your tendency to grasp your prey
in grip of steel, fast as a viper's
tongue, then hover over it,
waiting to see how things turn out.

Show me your hands
and I will tell you what you've done
for vanity, or luck, or something else:

for having had or not had love,
for having been good at things or not,
for having been expected to,
or just expecting,

for having probably been kind or
having possibly been cruel.
for having loved children

Men
  Women
or having been loved by all of them.

But on the other hand,
What does it matter anymore?

STEEPLECHASE

(*A reminder to my girls*)

I rode a roller coaster
long enough to know
there is a falling out

but didn't know it then
and never knew enough
to spread a safety net
below my good intentions

CIRCUS

After the bleachers have been
emptied of the roaring crowds,
a silence comes—a silence as
final as if imposed by
a deafened ear, as if holding
within itself the sum of
sadness from all our
yesterdays, feeling like
velvet feels when fingers
grope a wall encased in it,
searching for some egress,
a point that marks the place
where one can start to
break through to the light.

It is a silence so complete
and cruel that it evokes
our human helplessness and
taunts us with the ghosts
of past mistakes, of reckless
moments and of latent dreams,
a silence now made human by
its strange effect of sitting
on the heart until it shrinks
for want of momentary hope,
then closing like a mantle

on our grief.

After the bleachers have been
emptied of the cheering crowds,
the tightrope walkers gone
to less precarious lives,
the trapeze artist catching
hands no more, the end of
bidding for a rapturous
sigh, a gasp of horror, or
a show of nerves,

when all is gone that
elevated us to dare to hope,
to let our dreams run free,
the animals remain, content to
chew the grub that constitutes
the instinct's prime pursuit,
content to sleep without
the need to dream, to ride
upon the passing day as if
it were an hour, a year.
No matter: without fear
there's only peace.

After the bleachers have been
emptied of cheering crowds,
the clowns are left to shed
their greasepaint masks,
only to feel denuded of their

art and hear the silence
most of all.

BEFORE WORDS

Before words,
we know the smell,
   the feel of air,

   know how storms look,
know how deceiving
   Sun can be,
      how treacherous,

   know how
the wind can be
   A tyrant.

   After words,
we are diminished
in the telling
   of it.

   Asked,
we say we have
forgotten things,
   or never knew them,

   or that,
lacking words,
   they never did exist.

JUST WHEN

The brain is more than all of us,
Much more than we can know,
And in the darkness of the night
From it black thoughts can flow.

And just when it is time to sleep,
To give our hearts a rest,
It summons up the worst of dreams
To dim what we've done best.

Do duties of a menial sort
Or of high cerebration
In order to democratize
The brain, our ruling nation.

Do anything and everything
In search of parity:
No use! We are conditioned
To a sort of slavery

In which we *think* we know ourselves
(But know we do not know)
And manufacture fodder
For that brain, which then will grow

To something more tyrannical

Than we could ever be.
We are transfixed, encaptured by
An abject misery,

So that, when limbs and lips and eyes
Seek solace in the night,
Our wrongs loom large and obfuscate
The times that we've been right,

Loom larger than our hearts can bear,
Arrange our memory
So that the woven patterns there
Become our destiny.

GEOMETRY

Thought
like threads of steel
can redesign the structure
of society

or be a tightrope
upon which to balance
impulsivity and reason

or a railing
to assure safe passage through
the roller coaster rides

or, where the muddy waters swirl
and hope is twisted into
tangled ganglia, thought can
strangle

like a rope garotte

ENDURANCE

At this certain age
our task is to endure
against a tide of malady,
great loss,

a singular, compelling urge
to crawl between the covers
where some comfort lies.

Why to endure?
To catch a beam of happiness
before it disappears;

be thought of
as reliable and strong;
conquer, day by day
our fear of something

that might be the heaven
we have sought on Earth.

OUTDISTANCED

Outdistancing
my old commuter train
I put my gear in neutral,
catch my breath,
exhilarated.

Down below me,
chugging steadily,
the iron horse beats out
an epitaph:

re mem ber me re mem ber me.

NDEX OF TITLES